Cock-a-doodle-doo!

Cock-a-doodle-doo!

A first book of farm animals

Venice Shone

ORCHARD BOOKS

For Danny

ORCHARD BOOKS
96 Leonard Street, London EC2A 4RH
Orchard Books Australia
14 Mars Road, Lane Cove, NSW 2066
First published in Great Britain 1991
© Text and illustrations Venice Shone 1991
The right of Venice Shone to be identified as author and illustrator
of this work has been asserted by her in accordance with the
Copyright, Designs and Patents Act, 1988.
A CIP catalogue record for this book is available from the British Library.
1 85213 269 8 (hardback)
1 85213 322 8 (paperback)
Printed in Belgium

Cock-a-doodle-doo!
The cock is crowing.
The day is beginning.

Here comes the sun,

rising over the hill.

All around the farm

the animals are waking.

The cows are mooing.

It is milking time!

Down in the field

the lambs are playing.

High on the hill

the farmer is working.

Over in the orchard

the rabbits are hopping.

Close by in the yard

the hens and geese are pecking.

The goat is in the garden

where the vegetables are growing.

The pigs in their sty are

feeding and wallowing in mud.

Here comes the rain!

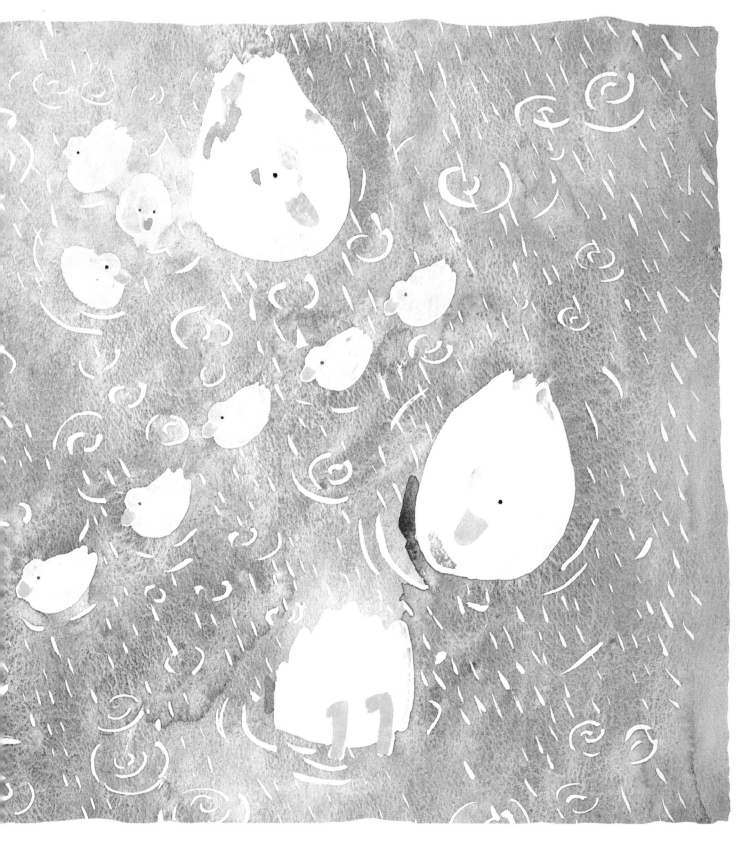

The ducks are happy splashing.

The horses in the stable

are warm and dry.

Now the day is ending.

The cows are coming home.

In the darkness outside
the owl is calling.

Too-whit-too-whoo!

The farm cat and dog
are safe and snug inside.
Goodnight!